Why Did God Make Me a Boy?

Authors: **Joe Owen** and **Abby Owen**

Illustrators: **Justine Foster** and **Omar Gamboa**

a product of Answers in Genesis

ISBN: 978-1-9844-1194-5
SKU: 10-1-891

Authors: Joe Owen, Abby Owen
Illustrators: Justine Foster, Omar Gamboa
Layout Designer: Justine Foster
Editors: Evonne Krell, Ryan Freeman, Sarah Zornes
Production Design: Dan Zordel, Shonda Snelbaker, Joel Leineweber, Jenn Reed,
Viviann Carlson and Michaela Duncan

Printed in China.

Why is it so important to read this book to your children?

The beginning of the twenty-first century was permanently marked by the explosion of gender ideology in the media, social networking, and school curricula around the world. It seems that the promoters of the sexual revolution will not rest until they eradicate God's design for men and women. However, just as in all of church history, false teaching has obligated the church to define what Scripture really teaches about important doctrines. Today, we are being challenged to return to the theology of biblical manhood and womanhood. Let's take the utmost advantage of this opportunity!

The books *Why Did God Make Me a Girl?* and *Why Did God Make Me a Boy?* were written by Joe Owen and his daughter Abby Owen, who are both part of the Latin American ministry of Answers in Genesis.

Their purpose is to support parents not only in countering the bombardment of gender ideology to their homes but also in teaching children about how God wants to glorify himself through their respective manhood or womanhood.

Because no one has lived fully in accordance with God's plan, purpose, and design, these books also present the message of salvation through Jesus Christ. It is only through Jesus that we can live out the structural and functional aspects of the image of God in us. To learn more on this topic, please visit **AnswersInGenesis.org** for additional resources.

God tells us in his word that he created the universe in six days.

On the first day, he created the earth (our home!) and the space of the universe. Outer space didn't have any stars yet, and the earth didn't have the mountains, oceans, animals, plants, and humans like it has now.

Everything was dark, but God was about to change that. God had a plan to give light just as he has a plan and purpose for every part of his creation.

On the first day,
God made the light,
and it shone on the earth.

On the second, third, and fourth
days of creation, God made the air and sky,
the seas, the land, and the plants on the earth.
Then he created the planets, sun, moon, and,
finally, the stars.

He made everything with a purpose.

On the fifth day, God made the sea creatures and the flying creatures. Can you imagine how amazing it would have been to see all the swimming and flying creatures come into existence by God's power?

Imagine the different types, shapes,

8

and colors of air and sea creatures!

On the sixth day, God made the land animals according to their kinds. Groups of animals all looked different from each other. God made them in sizes from big to small.

But God was not yet finished with his creative work.

What came next would be the most special part of God's creation!

Later on the sixth day, God made the first man and woman. These two creatures were made very different from the plants and animals.

They were made in God's image and likeness.

In these images, can you identify which is a woman, which is a man, which is an animal, and which is a plant?

What does it mean that people were created in God's image?

That is a great question!

We reflect some things about God like a mirror reflects some things about you. This does not make us equal with God because we are only part of his creation.

We are unique from any other part of God's creation because we have a spirit. We can talk with God and have a relationship with him. We can think, speak, write, create, and love.

God gave Adam the responsibility to lead and guide his wife and children.

That's why God gave Adam the command about which tree he should not eat from in the garden of Eden. Adam would also provide for, protect, and lead his family.

Eve was made to be a "helper" for Adam to carry out his roles. This did not mean that Eve was less important than Adam.

The different roles God gave Adam and Eve complemented each other, so they were better when they worked together.

Adam and Eve had children who grew up, married, had children, and so on. Eventually, the earth was filled with people! Everyone living today came from Adam and Eve.

This means that all boys and girls are made in God's image. Every person is important to God and a special creation.

Hi, I'm Joe!

There are ways we boys reflect qualities of God that are different from the ways that girls do. This doesn't mean that one reflects God better than the other, just that they are different.

How can two people reflect the same thing in different ways?

Here's an example. Let's say two friends are told to go to the same park and write down what they see. One friend may describe the animals and plants. The other friend may notice the pond and the tire swing.

Although both friends are "reflecting" how the park looks, they are doing it in different ways.

They are both right because the park has animals, plants, a pond, and a tire swing.

God has given both boys and girls different abilities, interests, and ways of thinking and doing things.

Like Eve, girls have the role of a helper. They also reflect God's caring nature for his creation in the way they care for their families, their friends, and creation.

Boys have some of the same roles as girls, but they have different ones too.

Like Adam, boys will have the roles of providing for, protecting, and leading their families one day.

Genesis 1–2 shows that Adam was given the leadership and responsibility for the creation, which would include his family.

The New Testament also teaches about the important leadership roles of men in both the home and church.

Today, some men give up or ignore their leadership roles in the home or church, while others use it in hurtful or selfish ways. But the Bible says that a man's leadership includes providing for, protecting, and serving those under him. A good leader loves, serves, and helps those in his care.

Provide

Protect

Teach

You are a special creation, and every part of being a boy is for God's glory.

One of the ways that boys reflect God is that many boys will someday be husbands and fathers.

Not every boy will become a husband or father, but many will. These roles are wonderful blessings from God. Someday many of us will have the opportunity to glorify God by providing for a family, protecting them, and teaching them about our wonderful Creator God and his plan of forgiveness in Jesus Christ.

Our families should see that although we are diligent in working to provide for them, our trust for provision is always in God.

The things you learn, the activities you participate in, and the way you act as a boy can prepare you for your God-given roles.

You Were Created in a Very Special Way!

Do you love a certain subject like math or music? You may one day use that in a job! Do you watch out for your brothers, sisters, teammates, or friends? You are being a protector! Do you love to draw or build things? You may use these skills to help and encourage others!

Some people think that certain activities and interests should only be for girls or boys. They may think boys shouldn't be artists or poets or that girls shouldn't play sports or become scientists.

This is not true! I am a man, and I love poetry. The psalms in the Bible were written by men. And many famous scientists have been women. Both boys and girls can glorify God by enjoying many of the same things.

It is important that our interests, whether art, building, music, cars, poetry, or sports, do not stop us from accepting and living out our specific roles as boys now or as men later.

Some people say that everyone can decide for themselves if they want to dress like a boy or a girl, regardless of what God created them to be. But God doesn't make mistakes.

He made each person either a boy or a girl for a reason.

Since God made the first clothes from animal skins for Adam and Eve after they sinned, people have created different clothing based on where and when they live. But in the past, men and women around the world have dressed distinctly from each other because they recognized their differences.

Ethiopia

Scotland

Venezuela

Jordan

Japan

In the Bible, God commanded women not to wear men's clothing and men not to wear women's clothing (Deuteronomy 22:5).

Today, boys and girls often wear similar kinds of clothing, like pants, shorts, and T-shirts.

But there are clothes that are only worn by girls or boys. So, it is not honoring to God for boys to dress in a way where they are trying to look like a girl on purpose. That shows a heart attitude that is rejecting God's design for who God created them to be.

Should we really do everything the same?

If being a boy is such a great honor, why do many people teach that boys and girls do not have differences?

To understand how this happened, we need to go back to the beginning when Adam and Eve rebelled and sinned against God. They disobeyed God's command and ate of the tree of the knowledge of good and evil.

Many things changed, and since then, we see the corruption of sin in God's creation. Not only do people suffer, but the whole creation also suffers. Many people try to ignore God because of the sin in their hearts.

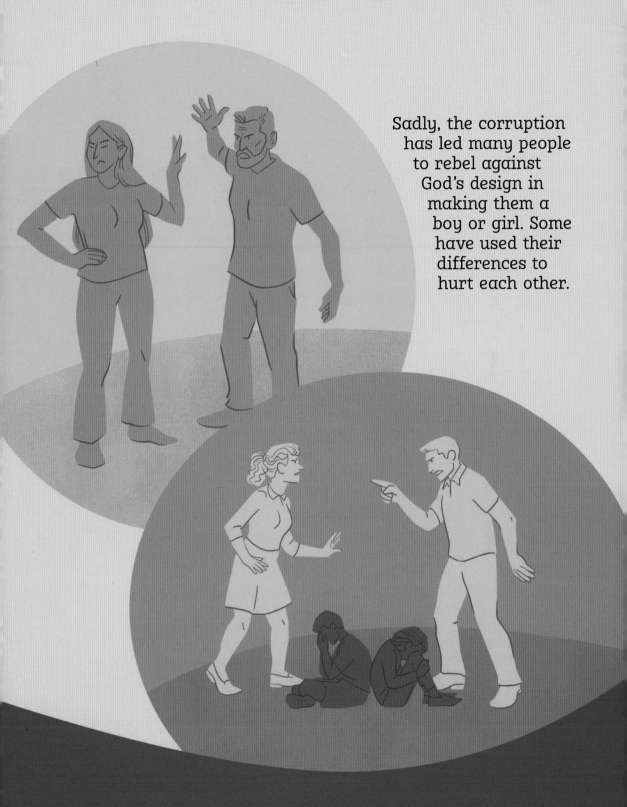

Sadly, the corruption has led many people to rebel against God's design in making them a boy or girl. Some have used their differences to hurt each other.

Some men are mean to women. And some women think that being a helper and mom is less important than doing other things.

People today have rebelled against God just like Adam and Eve. They treat each other in harmful ways that do not reflect God's love. Also, some are confused, and others reject God's perfect design for men and women.

This rebellion leads to pain and broken relationships between us and God and other people.

It seems as if there is no hope for us! But God had a plan to save us from our sin.

1 God the Father sent his only Son to the world as a baby.

2 Jesus grew from a baby to a man. But he never sinned because he is God.

5 Finally, God the Father brought Jesus back with him to heaven. Jesus will return someday for those who trust him!

4 Three days later, Jesus rose from the dead by the power of the Holy Spirit.

3 Jesus took the punishment for our sin on himself when he died on the cross.

You can be forgiven of your sins if you turn away from them and put your trust in Jesus to save you.

When you trust in Jesus, you become a child of God.
God has promised that Jesus will return one day for his
children, and they will rule in the new heaven and earth
with Jesus forever. All the bad things will be gone.

God always had a plan.

Have you turned from your sins and trusted in Jesus? Can you thank and praise God for making you a boy?

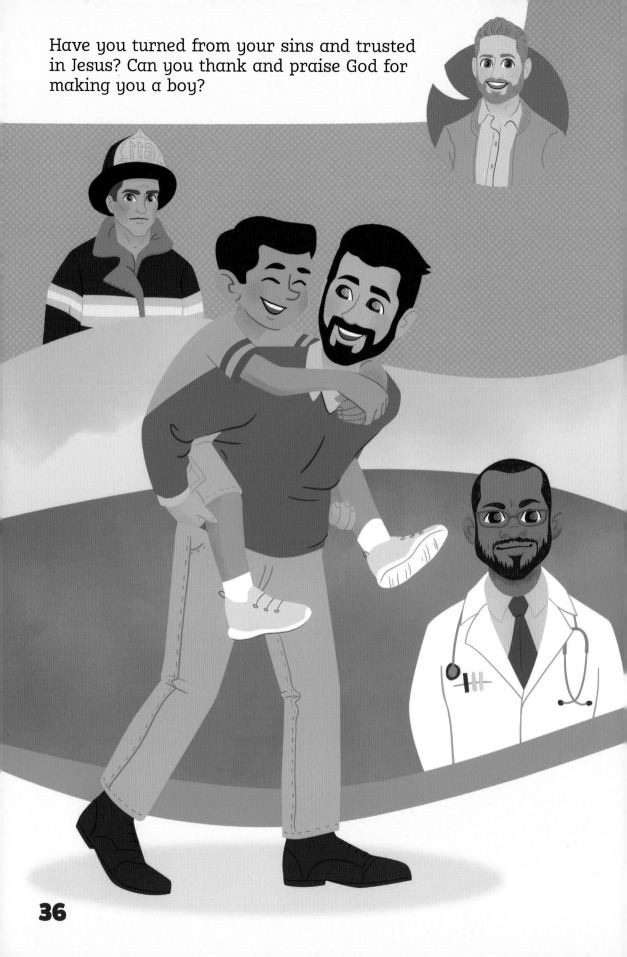

Being a boy is an awesome privilege! God has given boys the roles to one day provide for, protect and lead others. This includes the possibility of becoming a husband and father.

We bring glory to God when we accept the special roles God has given to men, even when we fulfill them in different ways by remaining single, getting married, or having children one day.

As boys, we can pursue the unique skills and interests God has given us. Whether you like sports or science, math or music, gardening or building, you can use these areas to honor God, knowing that he has a plan just for you.